TEACH YOUR CHILD
TO READ
PROPERLY

59 PD

$\frac{6}{11}$

In the same series

Help Your Child With The New Maths
555 Ways To Amuse A Child

Uniform with this book

TEACH YOUR CHILD TO READ PROPERLY

by

Niels Madsen

PAPERFRONTS
ELLIOT RIGHT WAY BOOKS,
KINGSWOOD, SURREY, U.K.

Made and Printed in Great Britain by
Cox and Wyman Ltd, Reading, Berks

THE LESSONS

WORKSHEETS

Instructions to be given by the teacher, with one or two examples on a black-board. The child can either fill in the worksheets in this book or copy them out and complete them on separate pieces of paper.

INTRODUCTION

If you are looking for, and needing, a book to help you to teach reading, you have found it. It is in your hands.

It is perhaps a sad reflection on our times that one can no longer assume that children will be taught to read adequately in the course of a normal education. This book fills the gap. It enables the parent or another adult to set about teaching a child to read. The method is systematic, and is derived from my own experience.

After more than twenty years spent teaching reading to young children – first as a class teacher, and later as a Headmaster – and using various methods, I am convinced that this book provides an effective answer to much of the illiteracy found in today's schools and even found, regrettably, in the adults which the children grow into. The solution lies in a book of systematically arranged rules with hundreds of appropriate words, exercises, ideas and worksheets. This is precisely such a book.

I have taken it that there is one child to be taught, although it has been my experience that learning is helped if there is more than one child and if it can be turned sometimes into "games" they can play. However, given a child to be taught and an adult ready to teach, the only other requirement I recommend is a black-board, even a small one, and a prodigious supply of cards to be written upon.

Teaching a child to read by this method will not interfere in any way with formal education at school. Indeed, the assumption is that there may have been gaps in that education which led the parent to turn to this book to fill them. Literacy is the key to all education. Until the child can read, most of education is held back. By teaching the child to read, you unlock the door to the riches that education brings. You help the child with those important first steps along the road which he will tread for the rest of his life.

The method of teaching is equally valid for boys and girls. I have referred to the child as "he" for convenience to avoid the cumbersome "he or she" construction throughout. "He" should be taken to mean "she" in every instance where appropriate, as the book is, of course, just as suitable for anyone who is fortunate enough to have a female child! I should also say that this method will work with adults who suffer from the handicap of illiteracy.

Each letter of the alphabet has a "name" and a "sound", but it is the combination of the various "sounds" which makes the completed word, the word used in reading.

"Names" are used for "spelling" – "see ay tee" spells "cat".

"Sounds" are used for "word-building" (for reading) – "keh ah teh" *sounds* "cat".

I know that in some instances the combination of two or three letters makes a completely different "sound" from the "sounds" of the individual letters – for example, ph, sh, ay – but we must remember that we are teaching reading to beginners, and so lessons dealing with such combinations are to be found later in the book. (A teacher of mathematics does not teach quadratic equations to a pupil still learning addition of numbers.)

Once a child knows and can say the "sounds" of the letters – not the "names" – then the method of combining those simple "sounds" into word-combinations constitutes the basis of my Sound System of Teaching Reading; and believe me there *is* a method.

As ninety per cent of the words in the English Language begin with a consonant I have started my lessons with three-letter words which begin with a consonant.

I am convinced that this method of combining the "sounds" is the secret of successful teaching reading. The secret is in this book.

As you teach from this book and watch a child learn, the joy of teaching will be yours, and both you and the child will share the thrill of achievement. Go to it; I wish you happy teaching.

1

THE "SOUNDS" OF
THE LETTERS

Every letter has a name and a "sound".

We use the "sounds" when we read – so, teach the "sounds".

Here are the twenty-six letters of the alphabet, and the "sounds" they make when taken separately – note the word "separately".

Teach the simple, short, hard "sound" of each letter.

a. – sounds like the ah in ca t.
b. – sounds like the bch in be g.
c. – sounds like the keh in ca t.
d. – sounds like the deh in de n.
e. – sounds like the eh in egg.
f. – sounds like fff – (not feh as in the beginning of "feather", nor eff as in the beginning of "effort". "Fog" is not fchog – nor is it eff-og. It is fffo g).
g. – sounds like the geh in get.
h. – sounds like the heh in hill.
i. – sounds like the ih in ink.
j. – sounds like the jeh in jelly.
k. – sounds like the keh in kick. (This keh is often called the "kicking keh" to distinguish it from the keh at the beginning of ca t.)
l. – sounds like the leh in lily.

m. – sounds like the mmm in mum.

n. – sounds like the neh in net.

o. – sounds like the oh in cot.

p. – sounds like the peh in penny.

q. – sounds like the keh and weh together. (Kehweh as in the beginning of quick.)

r. – sounds like the rrr in rub.

s. – sounds like the sss in sister. (It is not seh. Sup is not seh-up.)

t. – sounds like the teh in ten.

u. – sounds like the uh in up.

v. – sounds like the veh in velvet.

w. – sounds like the weh in wet.

x. – sounds like ks in exit.

y. – sounds like the yeh in yet.

z. – sounds like the zzz in buzz.

2

SOME METHODS OF TEACHING THE "SOUNDS"

Before I name some of the methods, here are two *which must never be used*.

a. *Never* use Capital Letters.
b. When using a word-picture book, never say "ay" is for apple. It isn't, "ah" is for apple.

Use the "sound" not the name.

Method 1.
Print the letters, (the small ones, not the Capitals – most words in Reading Books are in small letters) – print the small letters as large as you can on *one* sheet of paper, and place it where it can be seen frequently throughout the day, for example in the kitchen. The child will see it as he comes in and out of the room. He will be saying the "sounds" as he waits to eat.

If the letters are on two sheets the child's eyes will have to move from one sheet to the other – *but* – if there is a pretty picture between them, or near them, the letters will seldom get looked at. Place the sheets next to each other.

Method 2.
Point to a letter, say the "sound" and then get the child to say the "sound" – not too many letters at one time, and don't always start with the same "sound". Start in the middle of the alphabet.

Method 3.
Point to a letter, say the "sound" and let the child say the "sound". Then point to other letters and let him say their "sounds".

Method 4.
Point to a letter, say the "sound", then get the child to say it. If there are two or more children, get them to take it in turns.

Method 5.
Let the child point to a letter and you say the "sound". Do this the other way round, with you pointing to a letter and him saying the "sound". (The child will never forget the letter he pointed to.)

Method 6.
Say a "sound" – then get the child to point to the letter "sounded". Repeat with another "sound". Then reverse roles.

Method 7.
Let the child feel over the letter with his fingers and then say the "sound" he has traced.

Method 8.
Get the child to copy some letters you print on the blackboard. Mix the letters every lesson and don't always start with "ah" or any particular "sound".

Method 9.
Let the child make coloured patterns with various letters.

Method 10.
Give the child plenty of copy work. (Children love to copy and are invariably proud of their efforts. Praise them. Let them enjoy learning – it will become easier and quicker.)

Method 11.
Print each letter separately on slips of paper. Put them in a box and have a "Lucky Dip" – the child has to say the "sound" he has picked out.

Method 12.
If there are two children, let each pick out a slip – and then exchange them. Now see if they can say the "sound" they have been given.

Method 13.
Get the child to write down the letters of registration from passing cars. Now see if he can "sound" the different letters. (This is a game you can play when out with him.) Or get him to collect letters from advertisements in magazines/ newspapers etc., and see if he can "sound" the different letters.

Aim to get the child used to *seeing* the printed letters – to *print* the letters himself – to *hear* the *"sounds"* of the letters – and to *say* the *"sounds"* of the letters.

Above all, praise every effort – you will be well rewarded.

3

PUTTING THE "SOUNDS" TOGETHER

When the child knows and can say the "sounds" of all the letters, he is ready to put some of them together and start word-building – *the first step to reading*.

Tell the child that the most important letters are:

a (ah)   e (eh)   i (ih)   o (oh)   u (uh)
and they are called vowels. (Do not labour the name.)

Print them on the black-board – *"sound" them* – ah   eh   ih   oh   uh.

Now tell the child that these letters alter the word – and that is why they are the important letters.

Print on the black-board –

ba g   be g   bi g   bo g   bu g.

(*Important. Do not* alter the letters already on the board – *do not* add letters *in front* of others. Print the five words.)

Now say them as they are printed:

ba g   be g   bi g   bo g   bu g   *fastening the first letter to the vowel following.*

Do not, repeat *do not* say them like this, bag, beg, big, bog, bug.

You must fasten the first letter to the vowel following.

ba g   be g   bi g   bo g   bu g.

This fastening of the first two letters is of vital importance.

Once this fastening rule has been established you are ready to start word-building with words of three letters: a consonant, a vowel, a consonant.

Many of today's poor readers are poor readers because they have not been taught the correct way of word-building.

There is only one correct way, and here it is:

1.   Always start with the "sound" of the letter at the beginning of a word and read across to the right.
   (This may seem common sense to you, but it's surprising how many children look anywhere in the word for a "sound" they readily know, and start from there. Is this the answer to poor spelling?)

2.   Always fasten the first letter to the vowel following – e.g.,

   pat is sounded pa t   bed is sounded be d
   pin is sounded pi n   cot is sounded co t
   rug is sounded ru g

(Try this for yourself. How do you say the word "strap"? Do you say s trap, st rap str ap or stra p? The correct way is stra p, with the vowel fastened to the consonants in front of it – but it will be quite a while before you start teaching words that begin with three consonants.)

Before I give you a list of three-letter words, let me repeat
the two golden rules for word-building:

a) Start with the letter on the left of the word.
b) Fasten it to the vowel following.

I repeat: *Never add a letter to the front of a word to form*
a new word.
"at" with a "p" does not say "pat" – it says "atp".
"at" with a "c" does not say "cat" – it says "atc".

Slow learners will look for a part they know and then add
the rest to the end of the word – this must result in poor
spelling.

Here is your first list of three-letter words. They are all
nouns and can be "pictured", and for your convenience
they are arranged in alphabetical order – alphabetical as
well as vowel.

Take them one set at a time.

Let the child see them on the black-board, or on a large
sheet of paper – let him *see them, hear them, say them,*
copy them – many times.

1. ba g ba t
    ca b ca n ca p ca t
    da d
    fa n
    ga g ga p
    ha m ha t
    ja m
    la d la p
    ma n ma p ma t
    pa d pa n
    ra g ra t
    va n

2. be d
    de n
    he m   he n
    je t
    ke g
    le g
    me n
    ne t
    pe g   pe t   pe n
    we b

3. bi b   bi n
    fi g   fi n
    hi m   hi p
    ji b
    ki d   ki t
    li d   li p
    pi g   pi n   pi p   pi t
    ri b   ri m
    ti n
    wi g

4. bo x
    co g   co t
    do g   do t
    fo g   fo x
    ho g
    lo g
    mo b   mo p
    po d   po p   po t
    ro d
    to p

5. bu d   bu g   bu n
    cu b   cu t   cu p
    gu m   gu n
    hu t
    ju g
    mu d   mu g

nu n   nu t
pu p
ru g
su m   su n
tu g   tu b

Here are most of the three-letter words to be found in the Oxford Dictionary. Use them as you did the previous lists, – let the child see them, hear them, say them and copy them. Children love to copy words.

(Remember to "sound" or read the words with the first letter fastened to the vowel following. Stress this – and note that no word ends with a "y" or a "w" or an "e" for those letters alter the short "sound" of the vowel – e.g., say, sew, toe.)

1. ba d   ba g   ba n   ba t   ca b   ca d
    can   cap   cat   dab   dad   fag
    fad   fan   fat   gag   gap   had
    hag   ham   hat   jab   jam   lad
    lap   mad   mam   man   map   nab
    nag   pad   pan   rag   ram   sad
    sag   tab   tag   van   vat   wax
    sat

2. be d   be g   be t   de n   fe d   fe n
    get   hem   hen   jet   keg   led
    leg   let   men   met   net   peg
    pen   pep   pet   red   set   ten
    vex   web   wed   yes   yet

3. bi b   bi d   bi g   bi n   bi t   di d
    dig   dim   din   dip·   fib   fig
    fin   fit   hid   him   hip   his
    hit   jib   jig   kid   kin   kip
    kit   lid   lip   mid   mix   nip
    pig   pin   rib   rid   sin   sip
    tin   tip   vim   wig   win   pip
    pit   rig   rim   rip   sit   six

4.　bo b　bo g　bo x　co b　co d　co g
cot　cox　dog　dot　fob　fog
fop　fox　god　got　hob　hod
hog　hop　hot　job　jog　jot
lob　log　lop　lot　mob　mop
not　nod　pod　pop　pot　rob
rod　rot　sob　sop　top　tot

5.　bu d　bu g　bu n　bu t　cu b　cu t
cup　dub　dud　dug　fun　gum
gun　hub　hug　hum　hun　hut
jug　jut　lug　mud　mug　nun
nut　pub　pug　pun　pup　rub
rug　rum　run　rut　sub　sud
sum　sun　sup　tug　tub

Tell the child that names are special words and that they begin with a capital letter – *but* – that the capital letters have the same "sound" as their small ones.

e.g.,　Da n　Pa m　Sa m　Bo b　Te d　Be n
Tom　Tim　Peg　Meg　Jim　Kit
Pat.

Here are a few words beginning with a vowel:

am　an　at　if　in　it　on　ox　up

A word of warning. Never – repeat never build a two-letter word into a three-letter word by adding a letter to the front, e.g., "p" added to the front of "an".

Always print the full word. If you want to add a letter put it at the end, e.g., do t　do g.

Get the rule of word-beginnings – (first letter and vowel fastened together) firmly fixed in the child's mind.

1. Cover up the last letter of a word and as the child says the beginning of the word uncover the last letter and let him say the complete word.

2. Let him start a word-book, collecting simple words which have the same beginnings.

   Make some of the lessons into games, and make them so that the child wants to play the game.

3. Give the child a letter printed on a card, place groups of two letter-cards around the room, and then let the child move around and see which three cards can make a three-letter word. (Don't give him the same letter every time.)

4. Let him find words in simple books around the home, or in the simple children's comics and magazines.

5. You say a word and then challenge the child to find it in the room.

At some time or other it will be advisable and helpful to keep a record of the child's progress. Now is the time to start. You will soon find out where help is needed and when headway is being made.

Above all – encourage, encourage and again encourage. A word of praise, a pleasant smile, and the child is in seventh heaven.

4

PUTTING THE WORDS TOGETHER

Once the child has mastered the "sounds", and can put them into simple words, he is ready for sentence-building. At this point, show him that every sentence begins with a capital letter, as do all names (see page 24). The word "I" is always a capital too. Tell him that names and the word "I" *always* have capitals, not only when they start sentences.

Before you begin putting words together, you *must* teach the child these words:

I   on   the   of   is   it   an   and

They are the most often used words in everyday speech.

Print them on a sheet of paper and pin it up in the kitchen. Use the words and point to them three or four times every day. Make the learning of these words easier by introducing them into simple sentences, and here are some with which to begin. (Some of them are "silly sentences". When the child finds them funny, laugh along with him. It helps learning – and teaching.)

1. Dad is mad.
2. Mum is not.
3. I am not mad.
4. I am a bad lad.

5. The cat is wet.
6. Get the tub.
7. Mum is at the tub.
8. Can the cat run?
9. The dog can run.
10. I can run.
11. The dog is on the bed.
12. I am on the bed.
13. It is a bad dog.
14. Pip is a pup.
15. Pip can run.
16. Is the sun hot?
17. The sun is hot.
18. The lid of the pan is hot.
19. Put the pan lid on the pig.
20. Put the pig in the pot.
21. It is fun to run.
22. Put the peg on the lid.
23. Can the man hit the lad?
24. The man can hit the lad.
25. The lad can hit the man.
26. The dog bit the bad man.
27. Hop on the rug.
28. The rug is wet.
29. Ned is a bad cat.
30. It bit Bob.
31. Peg is wet.
32. Can mum hem the bag?
33. Mum can hem the bag.
34. The man sat on the log.
35. It is a big log.
36. Ted and Tom got wet.
37. Rub the mug.
38. It is a red rug.
39. Hop up on to the van.
40. The lid is on top of the hot pot.
41. Rip and Rob did vex Kit.
42. I am not fat, am I?
43. Dad did win the bat.

44. Did dad win the bat?
45. Put the lid on the top of the pot of jam.
46. Rex is a dog, but Rob is a cat.
47. Is the fan on the cot?
48. The fan is on the cot.
49. The bat is in the bag.
50. The fat pig is wet.
51. The dog bit the rat.
52. The rat bit the cat.
53. The cat bit the dog.
54. Ken is not a pal of Ben.
55. Ron is a pal of Jim.
56. Sam is a pal of Ben.
57. Bob is a sad boy.
58. Dan is not sad.
59. The lid of the top tub is red.
60. Tim and Tom had a lot of fun in the jet.

1. Use the sentences alternating them with sentences in other picture-word books. Use the lesson as a copying lesson – look for clear letters – a printing lesson.

2. Print the sentences on separate slips of paper, and have a "Lucky Dip".

3. Challenge the child to read the sentence that he has pulled out.

4. If you have two or more children learning, let each one challenge the others to read a sentence that he has pulled out.

5. Write down the registration letters of cars and see if the child can make words or sentences with these letters, e.g., E148 BIF – sentence: *Bob is fat.*

6. Give the child words on cards, and see if he can arrange three or four of them to form a sentence.

7.   Let the child make up "silly sentences" by using words from the other sentences, e.g. Tom (36) is in the (49) pot of jam (45).

     Children enjoy making "silly sentences" – laugh with them. It will add to the enjoyment, and the desire to read.

     Encourage them – it pays dividends.

WORKSHEET 1

Say and copy each word 3 times.

ba d   _____   _____   _____

ba g   _____   _____   _____

bat   _____   _____   _____

be d   _____   _____   _____

be g   _____   _____   _____

bet   _____   _____   _____

bi b   _____   _____   _____

bi d   _____   _____   _____

bi g   _____   _____   _____

bi n   _____   _____   _____

bit   _____   _____   _____

bo b   _____   _____   _____

bo g   _____   _____   _____

box   _____   _____   _____

bu d   _____   _____   _____

bu g   _____   _____   _____

bu n   _____   _____   _____

but   _____   _____   _____

WORKSHEET 2

Say and copy each word 3 times.

ca b   _____   _____   _____

ca d   _____   _____   _____

ca n   _____   _____   _____

ca p   _____   _____   _____

cat   _____   _____   _____

co b   _____   _____   _____

co d   _____   _____   _____

co g   _____   _____   _____

co t   _____   _____   _____

cox   _____   _____   _____

cub   _____   _____   _____

cut   _____   _____   _____

WORKSHEET 3

Say and copy each word 3 times.

da b _____ _____ _____

da d _____ _____ _____

de n _____ _____ _____

di d _____ _____ _____

di g _____ _____ _____

di m _____ _____ _____

di n _____ _____ _____

dip _____ _____ _____

WORKSHEET 4

Say and copy each word 3 times.

fa d　　　_____　　_____　　_____

fa g　　　_____　　_____　　_____

fan　　　_____　　_____　　_____

fat　　　_____　　_____　　_____

fed　　　_____　　_____　　_____

fen　　　_____　　_____　　_____

fib　　　_____　　_____　　_____

fig　　　_____　　_____　　_____

fin　　　_____　　_____　　_____

fit　　　_____　　_____　　_____

fob　　　_____　　_____　　_____

fog　　　_____　　_____　　_____

fop　　　_____　　_____　　_____

fox　　　_____　　_____　　_____

fun　　　_____　　_____　　_____

WORKSHEET 5

Say and copy each word 3 times.

gag _____ _____ _____

gap _____ _____ _____

get _____ _____ _____

got _____ _____ _____

gum _____ _____ _____

gun _____ _____ _____

WORKSHEET 6

Say and copy each word 3 times.

had   _____   _____   _____
ham   _____   _____   _____
hat   _____   _____   _____

hem   _____   _____   _____
hen   _____   _____   _____

hid   _____   _____   _____
him   _____   _____   _____
hip   _____   _____   _____
hit   _____   _____   _____

hob   _____   _____   _____
hod   _____   _____   _____
hog   _____   _____   _____
hop   _____   _____   _____
hot   _____   _____   _____

hum   _____   _____   _____
hub   _____   _____   _____
hun   _____   _____   _____
hut   _____   _____   _____

WORKSHEET 7

Say and copy each word 3 times.

jab _____ _____ _____

jam _____ _____ _____

jet _____ _____ _____

jib _____ _____ _____

jig _____ _____ _____

job _____ _____ _____

jog _____ _____ _____

jot _____ _____ _____

jug _____ _____ _____

jut _____ _____ _____

WORKSHEET 8

Say and copy each word 3 times.

keg   _____   _____   _____

kid   _____   _____   _____

kin   _____   _____   _____

kip   _____   _____   _____

kit   _____   _____   _____

WORKSHEET 9

Say and copy each word 3 times.

lad   _____   _____   _____

lap   _____   _____   _____

led.   _____   _____   _____

leg   _____   _____   _____

let   _____   _____   _____

lit   _____   _____   _____

lip   _____   _____   _____

lob   _____   _____   _____

log   _____   _____   _____

lop   _____   _____   _____

lot   _____   _____   _____

lug   _____   _____   _____

WORKSHEET 10

Say and copy each word 3 times.

mad   _____   _____   _____

man   _____   _____   _____

map   _____   _____   _____

mat   _____   _____   _____

men   _____   _____   _____

met   _____   _____   _____

mix   _____   _____   _____

mob   _____   _____   _____

mop   _____   _____   _____

mud   _____   _____   _____

mug   _____   _____   _____

WORKSHEET 11

Say and copy each word 3 times.

nag _____ _____ _____

nap _____ _____ _____

net _____ _____ _____

nip _____ _____ _____

not _____ _____ _____

nod _____ _____ _____

WORKSHEET 12

Say and copy each word 3 times.

pad   _____   _____   _____
pan   _____   _____   _____

peg   _____   _____   _____
pen   _____   _____   _____
pep   _____   _____   _____
pet   _____   _____   _____

pig   _____   _____   _____
pin   _____   _____   _____
pit   _____   _____   _____
pip   _____   _____   _____

pod   _____   _____   _____
pop   _____   _____   _____
pot   _____   _____   _____

pug   _____   _____   _____
pub   _____   _____   _____
pun   _____   _____   _____
pup   _____   _____   _____

WORKSHEET 13

Say and copy each word 3 times.

rag   _____   _____   _____

ram   _____   _____   _____

ran   _____   _____   _____

red   _____   _____   _____

rib   _____   _____   _____

rid   _____   _____   _____

rob   _____   _____   _____

rod   _____   _____   _____

rot   _____   _____   _____

rub   _____   _____   _____

rug   _____   _____   _____

rum   _____   _____   _____

run   _____   _____   _____

rut   _____   _____   _____

WORKSHEET 14

Say and copy each word 3 times.

sad   _____   _____   _____

sag   _____   _____   _____

sat   _____   _____   _____

set   _____   _____   _____

sin   _____   _____   _____

sip   _____   _____   _____

sit   _____   _____   _____

six   _____   _____   _____

sob   _____   _____   _____

sop   _____   _____   _____

sub   _____   _____   _____

sud   _____   _____   _____

sum   _____   _____   _____

sun   _____   _____   _____

sup   _____   _____   _____

WORKSHEET 15

Say and copy each word 3 times.

tab   _____   _____   _____

tag   _____   _____   _____

ten   _____   _____   _____

tin   _____   _____   _____

tip   _____   _____   _____

top   _____   _____   _____

tot   _____   _____   _____

tub   _____   _____   _____

tug   _____   _____   _____

WORKSHEET 16

Say and copy each word 3 times.

van   _____   _____   _____

vat   _____   _____   _____

vex   _____   _____   _____

wax   _____   _____   _____

web   _____   _____   _____

wed   _____   _____   _____

wet   _____   _____   _____

yet   _____   _____   _____

5

WORDS BEGINNING WITH TWO CONSONANTS

When a word begins with two consonants, the rule of fastening the vowel to the preceding letter – in this case letters – still applies. It is vital.

drum is sounded like dru m
skin is sounded like ski n
step is sounded like ste p

Here are a few words, split to show the correct way of sounding (reading) them.

sla p	sna g	sta b	gla d	cla p	bra t
ste m	fre t	ste p	spe d		
spi t	ski n	tri m	dri p	swi m	ski d
sto p	plo t	pro p	dro p	clo g	fro m
plu m	slu g	slu m	stu n	dru m	gru b

Now a few simple sentences.

1. Step up on the drum.
2. Fred is a glad lad.
3. The crab can swim.
4. Stop and grab a plum.
5. Did Bob and Ben stop the pram?
6. Tom can skin a plum.

Now some more split words. Print them on the blackboard, just as they are – split.

sla m   fle d   fli t   pra m   snu b   ble d
cri b   cro p   gra b   cra b   gri n   plo d
dra g   fla g

Get the essential "fastening" well schooled. It is vital.

Here are a few words not split. See if the child can say them correctly.

brat   bran   brag   clad   clam   clan   clap
crag   plug   spot   trot   grin   prig   stop
stag   drop   clod   swim   tram   grog   drug
brim   clip   clop

Now a few sentences with both three and four-letter words.

1. Drop the drum and prop up the pram.
2. The flag is on the top of the flat.
3. Put the crab on the mat.
4. Can Bat man stop on the spot.
5. Let the man get on the step.
6. Step up on to the top of the top step.
7. I am glad Stan did not get the drug.
8. Fred is at the tip of the drag net.
9. I am on the spot.
10. Pat did not grin at Pam.
11. It is a plus sum.
12. It is a trim ship.
13. Slap the big drum.
14. Do not stop the tram.
15. I am glad Trip and Trot got to the top.
16. Put the pram in the shed.
17. Stop that tap.
18. I can swim.
19. The crab ran up the prop.
20. I had plum jam.

Here's a game I played at least once a week and I think with some success.

See how many sentences the child can read correctly from a card. Print the score on your black-board. (Be careful with your cards. I heard of one child who "recognised" "aerodrome" from "aeroplane" by a thumb mark in the corner of the card.)
The score remains up until it is beaten – then the new score becomes the target. Print the new score on the black-board and let it remain there until the next time you play the game.

(Incidentally this is a good game to pay with multiplication tables – only *say* the question, don't put it on paper, e.g., "six sevens". "Four nines". And a little later on "How many sevens in forty-two?")

1. Try a few "silly sentences".
2. Have a "Lucky Dip".
3. Play group games.
4. Adapt any of the previous methods.

Progress may be slow – but it will come. Your record book will tell you where the problems are.

Have patience.

WORKSHEET 17

Say and copy each word 3 times.

bra t   _____   _____   _____

cla p   _____   _____   _____

cra b   _____   _____   _____

cla d   _____   _____   _____

cra g   _____   _____   _____

cra m   _____   _____   _____

drag   _____   _____   _____

glad   _____   _____   _____

pram   _____   _____   _____

slap   _____   _____   _____

stab   _____   _____   _____

snag   _____   _____   _____

stag   _____   _____   _____

tram   _____   _____   _____

WORKSHEET 18

Say and copy each word 3 times.

ble d   _____   _____   _____

fret   _____   _____   _____

sped   _____   _____   _____

stem   _____   _____   _____

step   _____   _____   _____

WORKSHEET 19

Say and copy each word 3 times.

clip   _____   _____   _____

drip   _____   _____   _____

grid   _____   _____   _____

grin   _____   _____   _____

grim   _____   _____   _____

prig   _____   _____   _____

skin   _____   _____   _____

skid   _____   _____   _____

spin   _____   _____   _____

spit   _____   _____   _____

swim   _____   _____   _____

trim   _____   _____   _____

WORKSHEET 20

Say and copy each word 3 times.

blob   _____   _____   _____

clog   _____   _____   _____

crop   _____   _____   _____

clop   _____   _____   _____

clod   _____   _____   _____

drop   _____   _____   _____

from   _____   _____   _____

grog   _____   _____   _____

plot   _____   _____   _____

plod   _____   _____   _____

prop   _____   _____   _____

stop   _____   _____   _____

trot   _____   _____   _____

WORKSHEET 21

Say and copy each word 3 times.

drum   _____   _____   _____

drug   _____   _____   _____

grub   _____   _____   _____

plum   _____   _____   _____

plug   _____   _____   _____

slug   _____   _____   _____

slum   _____   _____   _____

stun   _____   _____   _____

6

SIMPLE WORDS BEGINNING WITH "th", "ch", "sh"

This is the first lesson in which the combination of the first two consonants does not make the phonetic sound of each letter.

We now have new "sounds".

Take them slowly and remember to fasten the consonant combination to the vowel following.

Try these words.

tha t	the m	the n	thi n	thu d	chi p
cho p	cha p	chu g	chu m	cha t	sha m
she d	shi n	shi p	sho p	sho t	shu t
thi s	thu s	tha n			

And these sentences.

1. Shut the shop and chop the chips.
2. The thin slug is on the shed.
3. This is the man.
4. The thin lad is a chum of the fat lad.
5. Hit him on the chin.
6. That shop is shut.
7. He can skip.

When the child has really learned these "sounds", introduce the "wh". Show him how this combination of "w" and "h" is sounded backwards, like "hw". It is the only letter-combination that is.

"when" is sounded like "hwen"
"whip" is sounded like "hwip"

Try these: Whit   whim   wham

Do not mention the words "what" and "who". The "a" in "what" has not got the short "ah", and the "wh" in "who" is not sounded backwards.

A few more sentences.

1. I hit my shin on the thin box.
2. When is a chip not a chip?
3. When it is a chop.
4. I am glad I am ten.
5. Shut the shop, Sam.
6. The shop is not shut.
7. Put the pram in the shed.
8. That is a whip.
9. Hit the top and then run.
10. I did not chop the thin chips.

Print the words on separate sheets of paper. Give the child different sheets and see if he can say the words – then arrange them to form sentences.

Let him find similar words in his Reading Books.

Above all, let him copy and read. It leads to success.

WORKSHEET 22

Say and copy each word 3 times.

cha t   _____   _____   _____

cha p   _____   _____   _____

cho p   _____   _____   _____

chum   _____   _____   _____

chug   _____   _____   _____

sham   _____   _____   _____

shed   _____   _____   _____

ship   _____   _____   _____

shin   _____   _____   _____

shop   _____   _____   _____

shot   _____   _____   _____

shut   _____   _____   _____

that   _____   _____   _____

than   _____   _____   _____

them   _____   _____   _____

then   _____   _____   _____

thin   _____   _____   _____

7

THE MOST OFTEN USED WORDS

Here they are – the words most often used in our everyday speech.

I have arranged them in alphabetical order.

Print them on various sheets of paper and pin them up in a room.

Point to a word, say it, then get the child to say it.

Now another – then back to the first word.

Remember, this is a memory exercise – so repeat, and repeat. There is nothing to beat repetition as an aid to learning.

an	and	are	at	
be	but	by		
can				
did	do			
for	from			
get	go	got		
had	he	her	him	
I	if	in	is	it
me	my			
no	not	now		
of	on	over		

see	she	so		
that	the	their	them	there
they	this	to		
up				
was	we	well	were	what
when	where	who	will	with
you				

Take plenty of time with this lesson. It is a question of memory, and children's memories vary.

Split the words into groups and take one or two at a time.

Let the child copy them – give him plenty of copy work.

Remember – the child *MUST* know these words. Give him time – and practice.

Here are some sentences. They include words from this and the previous lessons.

1. Can you see the dog?
2. This is not my cap.
3. It is his hat.
4. When will you get there?
5. They sat on the rug.
6. See if you can hit this.
7. What is this whip for?
8. This is a slim shot gun.
9. I can do it if you can.
10. What will you do now?
11. He is not a thug, is he?
12. There you are then.
13. It is up to you.
14. Did you see that?
15. Go with them to that hut over there.
16. They put the boy on the top step.
17. It is a big drop from the top.

Take the lessons slowly, and repeat, repeat, repeat.

WORKSHEET 23

Say and copy each word 3 times.

an   _____   _____   _____

and   _____   _____   _____

are   _____   _____   _____

at   _____   _____   _____

be   _____   _____   _____

but   _____   _____   _____

by   _____   _____   _____

can   _____   _____   _____

did   _____   _____   _____

do   _____   _____   _____

for   _____   _____   _____

from   _____   _____   _____

go   _____   _____   _____

got   _____   _____   _____

get   _____   _____   _____

had   _____   _____   _____

him   _____   _____   _____

he _____ _____ _____

her _____ _____ _____

if _____ _____ _____

in _____ _____ _____

is _____ _____ _____

I _____ _____ _____

it _____ _____ _____

me _____ _____ _____

my _____ _____ _____

no _____ _____ _____

not _____ _____ _____

now _____ _____ _____

of _____ _____ _____

on _____ _____ _____

over _____ _____ _____

see _____ _____ _____

she _____ _____ _____

so _____ _____ _____

that _____ _____ _____

the   _____   _____   _____

them   _____   _____   _____

then   _____   _____   _____

there   _____   _____   _____

they   _____   _____   _____

this   _____   _____   _____

their   _____   _____   _____

to   _____   _____   _____

up   _____   _____   _____

was   _____   _____   _____

we   _____   _____   _____

were   _____   _____   _____

what   _____   _____   _____

when   _____   _____   _____

where _____   _____   _____

who   _____   _____   _____

with   _____   _____   _____

will   _____   _____   _____

you   _____   _____   _____

8

WORDS ENDING WITH
TWO CONSONANTS

In the previous lessons I have dealt with simple sounding words having phonic beginnings and endings – except those "must-be-remembered" words.

Sometimes however, the two consonants at the end of a word make a "sound" completely different from their phonic "sound" – so, *they are sounded together*.

(Try "sounding" the word "cash" phonetically. Impossible? – but not if you have taught the "sh" "sound" in an earlier lesson. Then it is not impossible – it is easy – ca sh).

As always, *fasten the first consonant or consonants to the vowel following* – and then *"sound" the last two consonants together*.

Although the child will not realise it, this is his first lesson in the correct splitting-up of words with two, three and even more syllables. A later lesson deals more fully with this correct method of splitting words. It not only aids reading but also aids spelling. But more about it later.

Once again I must stress the importance of taking each lesson slowly. Have patience – it pays. *Remember you are teaching a young child to read the printed word.*

(One fault I have against the "picture books", with a sentence underneath a picture, is that in time the children *do not read the printed words, they read the picture.* Try covering up the picture *before* the child can see it, and see what happens.)

Start as you mean to continue – do not take any other way but the correct one – *fasten the first consonant or consonants to the vowel following, and sound the last two consonants together.*

(Try saying the word "crash". Is it "c rash", or "cr ash", or "cra sh"?)

Now for some words. Some of them have one consonant in front of the vowel – others have two – but they all have two consonants at the end of the word.

ca sh	cra sh	sa sh	sa nk	ba nk
de ck	ne ck	pe ck	si nk	ri ng
wi sh	fi sh	di sh	lo ck	so ng
ro ck	mu ch	su ch	hu sh	ru sh

Now without the split:

flash	prank	rank	tank	sang	rang
bang	gang	pack	lamp	stamp	tramp
plank					
send	bend	fend	hemp	dent	test
best	west	peck			
wink	pick	sick	stick	silk	wing
gift	trick	link			
frock	song	lock	long	lost	
brush	sung	duck	jump	just	crust
trust	luck				

Now a few words with "tch" at the end – three consonants. Tell the child to forget the "t" and just sound the "ch".

ca tch	la tch	pa tch	fe tch	hi tch
di tch	pi tch	no tch	hu tch	cru tch

Try these sentences a few at a time.

1. Lick that stamp.
2. Do not rush the song.
3. Sing it as a sing-song.
4. Much cash is on the desk.
5. Put the lamp on the back of the pack.
6. The rest of the gang went on with the tramp.
7. Bang! went the gun and the men ran.
8. He shot the duck with his shot-gun.
9. Jump on the gang-plank.
10. Must you do that in this gift shop?
11. I am sick of this trick.
12. Can you lend me a silk hat?
13. We lost the match by six runs.
14. We went west with the King.
15. The ship sank.
16. Trust me to get the lock back.
17. There is a gold fish in the tank.
18. Just jump and trust to luck.
19. I did not wink at him.
20. The bell rang when he went into the shop.

If you make up more sentences remember not to use words ending with "e" or "y".

Use any of the previous methods of "getting the lesson over".

Let the child copy – it is a vital aid to learning (as is repetition in learning multiplication tables).

WORKSHEET 24

Say and copy each word 3 times.

cash _____ _____ _____
crash _____ _____ _____
sank _____ _____ _____
dash _____ _____ _____

deck _____ _____ _____
peck _____ _____ _____
neck _____ _____ _____
west _____ _____ _____
test _____ _____ _____

fish _____ _____ _____
ring _____ _____ _____
wish _____ _____ _____
sick _____ _____ _____

song _____ _____ _____
lock _____ _____ _____
rock _____ _____ _____

much _____ _____ _____
such _____ _____ _____
hush _____ _____ _____
rush _____ _____ _____
brush _____ _____ _____

9

WORDS WITH TWO VOWELS TOGETHER GIVING ONE "SOUND"

We now come to words with two vowels together – some
at the beginning of the word, e.g., aim;
some in the middle of the word, e.g., meat;
some at the end of the word, e.g., toe.

Teach this rule: *When two vowels come together in a word,
sound the first vowel by its name, and ignore the second
one – (and don't forget to fasten the vowels to the preceding
consonants if there are any).*

e.g.,   mai l   sea t   tie   roa d

(Note: there are some exceptions – they come later – see
page 115 for the alternative "sound" of the "ie" combination.)

Print these words on the black-board:

mai d – sound the "a" *name* – but not the "i"
eat   – sound the "e" *name* – but not the "a"
pie   – sound the "i" *name* – but not the "e"
goa t – sound the "o" *name* – but not the "a"

Some children will, of course, find words which do not
conform to this simple rule of *naming* the first vowel and
forgetting the second one – e.g., fuel, poet.

Do not tell them they are wrong. Tell them that there are some words which are different, and that you will show them some of those words, later – but for now just *name* the first vowel. Tell the children the correct sound of the words, (fuel, poet) and praise them for spotting the difference – and they'll never forget those words.

Now for a few words *beginning* with *two vowels:*

ail   aim   aid   eat   eel   ear   oat   oaf

Some words with *two vowels in the middle.*

grai n	sai l	rai n	slai n
hai l	trai n	mai l	pai n
stai n	mai d	wai st	Spai n
bea d	bea st	dee r	sea t
crea k	screa m	gree n	chea t
stea m	spea k	bea n	frea k
frie d	tie d	die d	crie d
trie d	spie d	roa d	foa m
boa t	coa t	soa k	coa l
toa st	floa t	groa n	

I mentioned exceptions – here's one – the "oo" as in "school" and in "stool", "fool", "cool", "shoot", "loot" and probably the most often used word "look".

A few words with *two vowels at the end.*

die	sue	hoe	toe
plea	due	foe	Joe
hue	three	tie	see
cue	pie		

Now for a list of words with the two vowels in various parts of the words.

leaf	meat	fail	road
three	sail	lied	see
toad	sea	rail	cried
deep	soak	read	wail
coat	green	seem	sleep
ail	weed	tried	feet
fleet	feed	moat	each
teach	cheap	laid	lie
week	pail	heat	aim
moan	steam	paid	roast
beef	raid	tied	toast
wait	groan	maid	main
hail	keep	cheek	seat
bead	free	spied	toe
goal	foal	steel	float
steal	nail	tail	train
tree	need	sweet	tie
eat	beast	beak	foe
boast	goat	peak	speech
coast	rain	Spain	plain
waist	grain	fee	flea
seek	teeth	speak	tea
meal	pea	died	doe
loaf	glee	leek	flue

Now for a few sentences:

1. He spied a train on the rail.
2. You must not steal the bead.
3. The leaf fell from the tree.
4. Speak up so that we can hear you.
5. Keep off the grass.
6. I must go to the coast.
7. Teach me to read.
8. He died from shock.
9. Can I tie the goat to the tree?
10. I eat toast and jam.
11. Wait for me near the sweet shop.
12. The rain in Spain is on the plain.

13. There must be a gas leak.
14. I hit my toe on the leg of the bed.
15. The rat had a long thin tail.
16. I sat on the wet seat.
17. You can speak to the man in the green hat.
18. The grass is green, and so are the weeds.
19. Mum cut the loaf and we had it for tea.
20. Why is the foal tied to the rail?

No doubt by now you have found out the best way of teaching – any of the previous methods which are proving successful.

WORKSHEET 25

Say and copy each word 3 times.

paid   _____   _____   _____

rain   _____   _____   _____

mail   _____   _____   _____

grain   _____   _____   _____

sail   _____   _____   _____

stain   _____   _____   _____

meal   _____   _____   _____

bean   _____   _____   _____

bead   _____   _____   _____

beast   _____   _____   _____

deer   _____

steam   _____   _____   _____

seat   _____   _____   _____

heat   _____   _____   _____

dear   _____   _____   _____

fried   _____   _____   _____

tied   _____   _____   _____

died   _____   _____   _____

spied   _____   _____   _____

tie   _____   _____   _____

coal   _____   _____   _____

coast   _____   _____   _____

road   _____   _____   _____

float   _____   _____   _____

toe   _____   _____   _____

fruit   _____   _____   _____

10

WORDS WITH
TWO SYLLABLES
– TWO "SOUNDS"

Up to now all your teaching has been concerned with words having *one* distinct sound. (The previous lesson dealt with words having two vowels together, but the combination of the two vowels gave just *one* sound.)

This lesson shows how to tackle words that have two vowels separated by one or two consonants.

e.g.,   travel   lesson   planted

Point out that each word has two separate vowels, giving two separate sounds.

Now, where do we separate the sounds?

Teach this simple rule:

If there is only *one consonant* between the vowels, split after the first vowel, e.g., ha bit.

If there are *two consonants* between the vowels split the consonants, e.g.,   Lon don   bul let.

There is much more to the splitting of long words, (see page 97) and to the separating of the sounds, than in this simple rule, but for the time being this rule will prove invaluable to beginners.

Once the child knows where to split a long word, and say it as it is split, he will not only become a more fluent reader, but his spelling will also improve.

Teach him that all long words are just a lot of short sounds put together.

(I realise that some of the words that I introduce here and later in the book are pronounced differently in the north and south of the country, e.g. "London" or "Luhndun"; "mother" or "muhther"; "brother" or "bruhther" – so be prepared for slight differences in the "sounds" of the letters from those "sounds" given on page 13. In particular, the southern "ar" "sound" which is heard in such words as "planted" ("plarnted"); "basket" ("barsket"); "command" ("commarnd").)

A few words – showing the split.

me tal	a mong	but ton	bas ket
can not	in sect	Scot land	Den mark
pea nut	in fant	pub lic	les son

Now a list of words – use a few at a time.

album	across	market	mustard
captain	British	sudden	seldom
seven	pelmet	helmet	Britain
Kenneth	kennel	began	bucket
distant	combat	afraid	gallon
petal	Briton	plastic	padlock
bullet	number	prison	fifteen
biggest	pretend	command	rubber
sandal	habit	rabbit	given
lemon	linen	listed	chicken
model	beaten	septic	London
rugby			

If you have a bright child, try him with these words:

e lec tric	se ven teen	hos pi tal
con so nant	A me ri ca	yes ter day
hap pi ness	Ca na da	Li ver pool
e ven ing	fol low ing	po lish ing

— SCUM ←

Let the child copy the words – a few at a time. I think you will find he will enjoy this lesson. He is now beginning to "read" long words. See if he can find some in his Reading Books – and what is more important "read" them.

The child will realise by now that every "sound" of a split word begins with a consonant.

Trouble? Oh yes – when children find words like "beautiful" and "photograph". I never attempted to split "beautiful". The children I taught used that word so many times (too many times) that they recognised it after one or two showings. (Admittedly, their spelling of the word varied considerably, but the "sound" was there, and that is what I was teaching.)

With the word "photograph" I told my children that the "p" and "h" together *usually* give the "short sound of 'f'" – and I would show them more later.

Now for some sentences.

1. I cannot go to the teashop.
2. Andy Pandy is in the shelter.
3. Ask for a packet of peanuts.
4. The bad man (cri mi nal) was sent to prison.
5. He is a prisoner.
6. We had to travel in seven different buses.
7. It was the biggest cannon he had ever seen.
8. This is a problem sum.
9. The model was presented with a medal.
10. He did not need the mustard.

11. The red red robin was fast asleep.
12. Can you reach the rubber stamp?
13. Can you say "afternoon"?

You know by now the best way of putting over your teaching.

WORKSHEET 26

Say and copy each word twice.

basket	_____	_____
cannot	_____	_____
gallon	_____	_____
market	_____	_____
rabbit	_____	_____
sandal	_____	_____
plastic	_____	_____

| lemon | _____ | _____ |
| kennel | _____ | _____ |

infant	_____	_____
insect	_____	_____
linen	_____	_____
distant	_____	_____
fifteen	_____	_____

London	_____	_____
pollen	_____	_____
model	_____	_____

button	_____	_____
rubber	_____	_____
rugby	_____	_____
bullet	_____	_____

11

WORDS ENDING WITH
THE LETTER "e"

Print these words on the black-board.

mad   her   rip   rob   cub

Say them and get the child to say them – point out the short "sound" of each vowel.

Now add an "e" to the end of each word.

made   here   ripe   robe   cube

Say them and get the child to say them – point out the different "sound" of each vowel – this time the "sound" is the "name" of the vowel – the long "sound".

We call the "e" at the end of a word, "the magic e" – because it alters the "short sound" of the vowel in the word, to the "long sound".

Teach this rule.

When a word ends with the "magic e", the vowel in the word "says its name".

Here are some examples:

fat	fate	Sam	same	mat	mate	cap	cape
her	here	pet	Pete				
kit	kite	hid	hide	bid	bide	fin	fine
hop	hope	cod	code	mop	mope		

And here are many more all ending with "the magic e".

nape	cape	fate	mate	take	late
game	came	safe	cake	name	wake
spade	shame	skate	plane	grape	shade
bake	cake	trade	brave	tame	
these					
gripe	like	nine	mine	time	bite
pine	dine	dime	fine	five	white
while	line	mile	tile	wide	drive
mope	dome	choke	smoke	stove	nose
sole	pole	dole	mole		
mule	cube	fume	plume	tube	ruse

Now for a few sentences to complete the lesson.

1. I like cho co late cake.
2. Peter bit into the cake.
3. He has five toes.
4. Did you see Kate and Steve dive into the bath?
5. Wake up. It is late.
6. Put on your cap and your cape.
7. It is wet in the lane.
8. The snake slid from the hole in the cave.
9. I have a fine thin pole.
10. Sam, wipe your feet on that same carpet.
11. Will the safe open wide?
12. Do not give fish-bones to the dog.
13. He made a slide on the slope of the path.
14. The con duc tor came for my fare.
15. The tree gave a lot of shade.
16. When A lad din rubbed the lamp, the slave came.
17. He had a plan of the plane.

WORKSHEET 27

Say and copy each word 3 times.

mat	_____	_____	_____
mate	_____	_____	_____
cap	_____	_____	_____
cape	_____	_____	_____
rat	_____	_____	_____
rate	_____	_____	_____
hat	_____	_____	_____
hate	_____	_____	_____
fat	_____	_____	_____
fate	_____	_____	_____
kit	_____	_____	_____
kite	_____	_____	_____
hid	_____	_____	_____
hide	_____	_____	_____
bit	_____	_____	_____
bite	_____	_____	_____

fin _____ _____ _____

fine _____ _____ _____

pin _____ _____ _____

pine _____ _____ _____

hop _____ _____ _____

hope _____ _____ _____

not _____ _____ _____

note _____ _____ _____

mop _____ _____ _____

mope _____ _____ _____

cod _____ _____ _____

code _____ _____ _____

cub _____ _____ _____

cube _____ _____ _____

plum _____ _____ _____

plume _____ _____ _____

tub _____ _____ _____

tube _____ _____ _____

12

WORDS WITH A DOUBLED CONSONANT IN THE MIDDLE

Print these two words on the black-board:

dinner   diner

Get the child to tell you the difference between the "sounds" of the words.

Anything else? Yes, one word has two "n's" in the middle.

Now teach this rule:

When a word has just *one consonant* in the middle the first vowel "says its name" – *"the long sound"*.

When a word has a *doubled consonant* in the middle the first vowel has the *"short sound"*.

Try these words.

sudden	label	bonnet	added	aided
winner	wined	filled	filed	timed
tiller	tiler	miler	miller	smiler
baker	manner	butter	butted	muted
mellow	seller	fellow	cooler	collar
tuning	running	sweetest	wettest	

At this point introduce the "y" at the end of a word – it has a sound similar to a "long e".

baby	tidy	pony	penny	foggy	jelly
rainy	dummy	giddy	sunny		

And the "ing" at the end of a word is always sounded together with the consonant in front of it.

ho ping	hop ping	swel ling	fee ling
wee ding	wed ding		

Now let the child look through his books and comics for similar words. Let him make lists of words with a doubled consonant in the middle, and put them into groups of a doubled consonant after "a" – after "e" – and so on.

There are of course, words which do not conform to this rule – and here are a few – "metal", "British", "seven", "prison", "habit", "given", "lemon", "linen" and "model" – but the child is now getting older and will learn to recognise them with experience.

WORKSHEET 28

Say and copy each word twice.

daddy   _____   _____

added   _____   _____

penny   _____   _____

jelly   _____   _____

wedding   _____   _____

giddy   _____   _____

digging   _____   _____

miller   _____   _____

foggy   _____   _____

sudden   _____   _____

sunny   _____   _____

mutter   _____   _____

mummy   _____   _____

muddy   _____   _____

13

WHEN TO "SOUND" THE LONG VOWEL

There are certain occasions when the "long sound" (the *name* of the letter) is used. Some of these have been covered already, e.g. when a word has the "magic e" at the end, and when there are two vowels together giving one sound, but here is a fuller list of rules to help the child know when the long vowel is "sounded".

When to sound the long "a"
1. When there is an "e" at the end of the word
    e.g., case cake tale.

2. When "a" and "i" come together in that order
    e.g., aim sail paid trail.

3. When "a" and "y" come together in that order
    e.g., day say pay stray.

When to sound the long "e"
1. When there is an "e" at the end of the word
    e.g., here these. (Not many like these.)

2. When two "e"s come together
    e.g., eel see feed bleed.

3. When "e" and "a" come together in that order
    e.g., eat beat plea team.

When to sound the long "i"
1. When there is an "e" at the end of the word
   e.g., line hide prize time.

2. When "i" and "e" come together in that order
   e.g., lie pie died fried.

3. When "y" comes at the end of a word which has no
   vowel
   e.g., fly try sky dry.

When to sound the long "o"
1. When there is an "e" at the end of the word
   e.g., bone home stone pole.

2. When "o" and "a" come together in that order
   e.g., coal boat coat toast.

3. When "o" and "e" come together in that order
   e.g., toe foe floe Joe.

When to sound the long "u"
1. When there is an "e" at the end of the word
   e.g., tube cute fume excuse.

2. When "u" and "e" come together in that order
   e.g., cue due blue.

3. When "e" and "w" come together in that order – and
   this is an instance when the "sound" of the combination
   differs from the "sounds" of the two letters
   e.g., few new stew dew.

Now for a list of words.

bay	hay	gay	way	claim	strain
plain	braid	grain	grade	shame	game
fail
seat	flee	fleet	deep	dear	deer

eat	three	thee	heat		
pry	my	tie	slide	file	mile
wine	twine	pride	kite		
roe	coast	rode	code	smoke	coal
moat	doe	toe	goal	foal	
blue	true	glue	few	flew	tune
cube	lute	cute	brute	newt	grew

This lesson lends itself to compiling lists.

14

THE "SOUND" OF
"er", "ir", "ur"

If you have faithfully followed the lessons in this book, your child will now know hundreds of words – and there are more to come – and how to "sound" them.

Print these words on the black-board.

her   sir   fur

Now say them.

Get the child to say them, and then ask if there is any difference in the "sounds" – (the "sounds", not the spellings).

Any difference? No. *So now we know that "er" "ir" "ur" have the same "sound".*

Here are some words to prove it.

her	sir	fur	herd	firm	surf
fern	dirt	cur	term	first	hurt
pert	stir	burn	turn	berth	birth
jerk	bird	purr	perch	curl	third
fir	slur	serf	surf	girl	turf
furl	stern	girth	spurt	nerve	twirl
verse	shirt	skirt	blur	mirth	hurl
swirl	spur				

A word of warning:

Do not have a Spelling Bee with the words of this lesson. *Remember you are teaching words which have the same "sound"* – but are spelt differently. Do not confuse your child.

Let him – *see* the words – *hear* the words – *say* the words, and *copy* the words.

He can arrange them into different spellings, but remind him that they have the same "sound"

Now a few sentences.

1. The boy politely said, "Sir".
2. Father gave mother a fur coat.
3. My brother is called Robert.
4. Roberta is the name of my sister.
5. The poor boy began to stammer and stutter.
6. He was a born fiddler.
7. The girl swimmer was the winner.
8. She came in first.
9. The rider turned and spurred his horse.
10. A deep cut hurts.
11. My sister puts curlers in her hair.

15

WHEN TO "SOUND"
THE FINAL "ed"

Print these words on the black-board:

added	aided	dotted	seated	glided
kissed	hugged	halted	dusted	passed
kicked	filed	cheered	pressed	

Now say them, and get the child to say them.

Now print them in two columns like this:

added	kissed
aided	hugged
dotted	passed
seated	kicked
glided	filed
halted	cheered
dusted	pressed

Say them – in columns – and point out: *The final "ed" is always "sounded" as another "sound" if it follows "t" or a "d".*

It is not "sounded" separately if it follows any other letter.

Try these:

hated.   "ed" follows a "t" – so "sound" it
hummed.   "ed" follows an "m" – do not "sound" it
added.   "ed" follows a "d" – so "sound" it
missed.   "ed" follows an "s" – do not "sound" it

Now for some words:

dotted	added	matted	mated
weeded	grated	kissed	named
seated	tested	crossed	pressed
hinted	wished	glided	halted
sifted	folded	dusted	blotted
rigged	hugged	fished	rusted
banded	posted	hooted	dented
kicked	fanned	famed	tugged
rested	begged	missed	rushed
hissed	patched	passed	pasted
potted	lifted	hemmed	talked
cheered	tanned	acted	filled
filed	spanned	hated	hatted
baited	dragged	scored	scared
scarred			

Here are a few sentences:

1. The girl kissed her mother.
2. Tom added the numbers together.
3. Richard subtracted the numbers.
4. The men cheered.
5. She dropped her purse into her bag.
6. Sam fished in the flooded pool.
7. The player rested after he had been kicked.
8. Susan used her blotting-paper.
9. Peter crossed the street and waited for Fred.
10. The snake hissed and the man fainted.

Try getting the child to use parts of various sentences and make "silly sentences". He will have to read the sentences to see which words he wants to use.

Here's one to start with:

The girl dropped the snake into her flooded bag and waited for Fred who had been kicked by the blotting-paper.

(Try it – or make two sentences out of it.)

WORKSHEET 29

Say and copy each word twice.

mated   _____   _____

matted   _____   _____

halted   _____   _____

rattled   _____   _____

rested   _____   _____

sifted   _____   _____

kissed   _____   _____

scored   _____   _____

crowded   _____   _____

sounded   _____   _____

blotted   _____   _____

tugged   _____   _____

rusted   _____   _____

16

THE "SOUND" OF "ght"

The child will have come across the combination of "ght" – and you can now tell him not to separate the letters but to combine them into the one "sound" of "teh".

Here are a few words:

fight   night   alight   straight   right
might   flight   bought

Now a few sentences:

1. It was a grand sight.
2. The pilot walked along the flight deck.
3. Bob was a naughty dog.
4. "Stand up straight," said the teacher.
5. The blazing house was well alight.
6. It is a dark night.
7. Bill was frightened.
8. The freight train rushed on through the night.
9. Hilda bought some sweets.
10. This is my right hand.

17

THREE SIMPLE RULES

1. *"c" before "e" is "sounded" like "s".*
   e.g., ace   face   rice   cell   ice   nice   race
         cent   lace   pace   dice   spice   mice   trace
         grace   place   police

2. *"g" and "dg" before "e" are sounded like "jeh".*
   e.g., page   lodge   age   gem   rage   badge
         budge   cage   dodge   sage   fudge   judge

Sometimes when "g" is followed by an "i" it has the soft "jeh" sound, e.g. "giant", "magic", "negligible" – but sometimes it has the hard "geh" as in "girl". By the time the child has reached this stage in the book he will recognise and be familiar with such words.

3. *The vowel before "dge" has the short sound –* (even though the word ends with an "e").
   e.g., edge   fudge   lodge

A few sentences:

1. He played the ace of clubs.
2. Can you trace the mice?
3. Tom was in a rage when he lost the badge.
4. Turn the page of the ledger.
5. It was a huge gem.
6. The helicopter hopped over the hedge.
7. He wore a black mask over his face.

8. It is not nice to trudge over the ice.
9. Germs in open cuts can hurt.
10. In a trice the prisoner was lodged in a cell.

Take the rules one at a time – and let the child find words in his Reading Books.

18

HOW AND WHERE TO
SPLIT LONG WORDS

This is one of the most important lessons in the book.

Teach it carefully and thoroughly – and wait for the results.
You should be more than satisfied.

The correct splitting of long words is the greatest aid to
more fluent reading – and spelling. Years of experience
have taught me that.

There are four simple rules.

1. *If there are two consonants between two vowels, split
   the consonants.*
   e.g., en ter tain ment yes ter day pon der

2. *If there is just one consonant between two vowels, split
   after the first vowel.*
   e.g., co mic fa na tic po pu lar

3. *Certain combinations have fixed sounds. They are never
   split.*
   e.g., ex un dis ght ly tion sion ing tch ph

4. *If a word ends with "le" the consonant before the "le"
   starts the last "sound".*
   e.g., sta ble ap ple raf fle a ble rat tle
   sim ple

Follow these rules and give the child plenty of practice.

Here are some long words. I have split the first few to show how and where. Split the others in the same way – or better still, get the child to split them. He will enjoy this and learn much in the process.

a du la tion	ca val ry	Cal va ry
ad mi nis tra tion	he li cop ter	e pi de mic
im per so nate	su pe rin ten dent	im per ti nent
im per ti nence	his to ri an	i ma gi na tion
im pri son ment	op ti mis tic	re vo lu tion
im pres sion	or na men ta tion	in te res ting

tomorrow	yesterday
moratorium	peculiarity
parenthesis	ragamuffin
responsibility	matriculation
sympathetic	sentimental
popularity	potentiality
preparation	presentiment
education	procrastination
recrimination	similarity
assimilate	benediction
capability	ceremonial
decapitate	escalator
furthermore	gravitation
humanitarian	impermeable
jurisdiction	kleptomaniac
locomotive	misunderstanding
negligible	oblivion
participation	recapitulation
stipulate	unemotional
versification	whimsical

Try a lesson of "saying and splitting". It is an old-fashioned method of teaching – but it gets results. Try it.

And now for a few sentences – and get your record-book out.

1. The wedding preparations were fascinating.
2. It is imperative that every child be given a satisfactory education.
3. Algebra and geometry are my best lessons.
4. There was a complete misunderstanding between the two players.
5. In my imagination I often recapture numerous exciting experiences.
6. Irresponsible persons are the main reasons for the disturbances at many political meetings.
7. The moon is many miles above our atmosphere.
8. Yesterday afternoon I visited the locomotive department.
9. The popularity of the jubilant entertainers is positively astonishing.
10. The Daleks, on television, have been almost completely eliminated.

Cuttings from newspapers, weeklies, comics etc. – complete with photographs of T.V. or Pop Stars, with information about or from the "Star" – make a "must" for the child. He will want to know what they have to say. Let him read the cutting. What child does not want to know the words of the song currently "Top of the Pops"? See if he can write out the song. The incentive is there – use it.

An easy dictionary is most useful – providing the child is allowed to use it (and it is not for display only). It could make a useful prize as a reward for him.

I have not mentioned anything about the child understanding what he is reading. Some of them will – others will need help. There are many excellent English books full of up-to-date comprehension exercises.

WORKSHEET 30

Say and copy each word.

te le vi sion   _____

television   _____

a du la tion   _____

adulation   _____

ca val ry   _____

cavalry   _____

Cal va ry   _____

Calvary   _____

he li cop ter   _____

helicopter   _____

e pi de mic   _____

epidemic   _____

ad mi nis tra tion   _____

administration   _____

sus pen sion   _____

suspension   _____

im per ti nent   _____

impertinent   _____

in te res ting   _____

interesting   _____

su pe rin ten dent   _____

superintendent   _____

re vo lu tion   _____

revolution   _____

la men ta tion   _____

lamentation   _____

mi sun der stan ding   _____

misunderstanding   _____

ob li vion   _____

oblivion   _____

op ti mis tic   _____

optimistic   _____

pre pa ra tion   _____

preparation   _____

Now split these.

combination   _____

education   _____

satisfactory   _____

imperative   _____

escalator   _____

yesterday   _____

sentiment   _____

remember   _____

individual   _____

19

WORDS ENDING WITH "tion" AND "sion"

Print these words on the black-board.

televi sion   ac tion   atten tion

They are everyday words. Say them – the child will recognise them.

Point out that "sion" and "tion" have the same "sound" of "shun" and are not split.

Here are more words:

option	nation	position
mention	pension	fraction
vision	motion	notion
session	tension	mission
passion	traction	proportion
lotion	abdication	abduction
elevation	explanation	infection
instruction	operation	detention
fiction	pollination	dispensation
confection	excursion	condensation
satisfaction	direction	affection
intrusion	construction	destination
destruction	extension	

And a few sentences:

1. It was an all-action boxing match.
2. We must pay attention to our teachers.
3. One of the detectives mentioned a name.
4. The mission to the station arrived on time.
5. Grandmother collects her pension on Thursday.
6. Nation shall speak peace unto nation.
7. At school we often read fiction stories.
8. The man gave no indication that he had seen the commotion.

20

THE "SOUND" OF "ou" AND "ow"

The letters "ow" combined in a word have two main pronunciations:

1. *As "sounded" in:*
   town   cow   how
   frown   brown   drown
   clown

Teach this "sound" to the child.

Then print the following words on the blackboard:

out   shout   cow   brown

Say them – and get the child to say them and show him that "ou" usually has the same "sound" as the "ow" "sound" of "how".

out	shout	pout	found
town	spout	house	mouse
round	count	couch	trout
sound	cow	brown	clown
frown	ground	mouth	drown
pound			

And a few sentences:

1. He found out about the stolen mouth organ.
2. This is the most renowned school in the town.
3. The milk from the cow did not turn sour.
4. He flung the trout on the ground.
5. A clown entertains at the circus.

(Note that whenever "c" is followed by an "i" it has a soft "sound".)

Of course there are exceptions to this: "ough" is a very complicated exception which defies analysis, with such words as "rough", "ought", "cough", "though", "through" and "thorough".

Parents/teachers will realise by now that this book is a 3–4 or 5 year course, depending on the ability of the child – and not a six months' crash course. By the time the child reaches this stage he will have met some of the exceptions to the various rules, he will be much older, and able to assimilate these exceptions; it's surprising how quickly children who have been taught correctly overcome the awkward exceptions.

In every walk of Life, there are exceptions to the Rules.

2. *"ow" also has the "sound" which is heard in the word "toe". Teach the child these words as examples.*
    low   mow   flow
    tomorrow   follow   sorrow
    blow   swallow   hollow

21

WHEN "r" FOLLOWS "a" OR "o"

Teach these "sounds" from the following words and sentences.

car	cart	yard	jar
far	harm	ark	card
hard	art	barn	tar
dark	lard	mark	sharp
star	shark	bar	lark
park	dart	artist	bark
farm	market	garter	
for	corn	fork	horn
morn	short	thorn	torn
port	fort	form	hornet
sport			

1. The car in the yard is for the scrap market.
2. Hark! Listen to the lark.
3. Come into the park.
4. Noah went into the Ark.
5. His coat is torn.
6. The star is high in the sky.
7. The jar of jam is in the larder.
8. It is morning.
9. Park the Ford in the yard.
10. It is a far better dart.
11. The artist sat on a form in the farm yard.
12. The ship turned and missed the shark.

13. It is dark.
14. The unicorn has a sharp horn.
15. The cart-horse is between the shafts.

22

THE SOUND OF
"oi" AND "oy"

As in the previous lesson, teach this "sound" from the words and sentences:

oil	boil	coil	foil
toil	join	coin	soil
hoist	joist	spoil	joint
moist	boiler	noise	rejoice
boy	joy	toy	coy
employ			

1. That shirt is soiled.
2. Boil the milk before making the custard.
3. Her eyes were moist with tears of joy.
4. Can you coil this rope?
5. Join us in a game of rounders.
6. We can employ a boy to look after the boiler.
7. The barrel was hoisted up.
8. Do not spoil the game by making a noise.
9. It is silly to destroy your toys.
10. Oil has been found under the North Sea.

There will, of course, be the odd exception to this rule, e.g., "stoic".

23

WORDS WITH
TWO VOWELS TOGETHER
GIVING TWO
SEPARATE "SOUNDS"

This is a lesson against the rules already learned – but you must not forget that your child is much older than when he first started learning to read, and should be more advanced in his reading ability and so able to assimilate exceptions.

At least, tell the child you think he is, and then he will try even harder – and what more do you want? A "trier" will eventually produce good results.

The child will learn to recognise the exceptions – you did.

Try these words:

fuel	poem	giant	poetry
idea	gruel	truant	duel
suet	diet	trial	pliant
reliable	triumph	reliant	

And these sentences:

1. The giant put some fuel on the fire.
2. Dial 999 for help.
3. My sister has to diet to keep slim.

4. It is cruel to fight a duel.
5. Tom is a reliable monitor.
6. The pianist played a minuet.
7. Reading poetry gives me much delight.

24

THE "SOUND" OF
"au" AND "aw"

Print these words on the black-board.

Paul	Saul	cause	Maud
gaunt	claw	yawn	fawn
straw	dawn		

Say them – get the child to say them. (Never mind the spelling, concentrate on the "sound" – the "sound" as in "all".)

Use these words:

haul	Saul	Paul	Maud
cause	bauble	caution	caustic
gaudy	gaunt	haunch	jaunt
saw	raw	straw	yawn
hawk	fawn	dawn	

Now these sentences:

1. Paul, please call Maud.
2. It was a drawn game.
3. The hawk mauled the mouse with its claws.
4. I yawn when I am tired.
5. Saul became known as Saint Paul.
6. I made a straw man.

25

THE LETTER "a" AT
THE END OF A WORD

When the letter "a" comes at the end of a word it has the "sound" of "eh". (But do not put too much stress on the "sound".)

Try these words:

opera	area	diploma
formula	gondola	banana
retina	vanilla	cholera
orchestra	hyena	arena
gorilla	panda	umbrella
stamina	algebra	spatula

And these sentences:

1. Helena listened to the opera.
2. Jane licked and liked the vanilla ice-cream.
3. Tarzan tamed the gorilla.
4. Use an umbrella when it rains.
5. You need stamina to run a long-distance race.
6. The hyena howled.
7. The gondola is used in Venice.
8. Philippa gained a diploma in Algebra.
9. The doctor suspected cholera.
10. This is a top-secret formula.

26

THE "SOUND" OF THE
"qu" COMBINATION

Get the child to look through various books – Reading and Reference – and find words with a "q" in them. See if he realises that "q" is always followed by a "u".

Now print these words on the black-board.

queen   squeeze   plaque   antique

Say them several times – then teach this simple rule.

The "qu" combination can have two sounds –
1. "keh-weh" – as in "quiz"
2. "keh" – as in "antique"

Use these words and sentences:

quilt	quell	quip	squint
quick	quiz	quench	mosque
quill	quack	quite	quiet
squeak	mosquito	quarrel	quiver
opaque			

1. The police quickly quelled the angry mob.
2. Alice saw a queer looking rabbit.
3. The King and Queen of Hearts often quarrelled.
4. The duck quacked and the mouse squeaked.

5. A mosquito is an insect.
6. Robin Hood took an arrow from his quiver.
7. Can you answer all the questions?
8. The Queen was seated at the antique desk.

27

THE "SOUND" OF THE "ie" COMBINATION

Sometimes the combination of "i" and "e" in that order gives the "sound" of "double ee".

Here are a few words:

field	priest	piece	shield
grief	yield	siege	thief
relief	brief	chief	fiend
believe			

And a few sentences.

1. The priest gave a brief sermon.
2. I do not believe that thief.
3. It was a relief to get home.
4. The chief held a meeting in the field.
5. May I have a piece of cake?

Here is a little chant – it may come in useful – (especially in spelling).

"i" before "e" – except after "c".

28

THE "SOUND" OF "ph" AND "ps" COMBINATIONS

Teach:
When "p" and "h" come together in a word, they make the "sound" of "feh".

"orphan" is "sounded" "orfan"
"phonetic" is "sounded" "fo-ne-tic"

Here are some words:

phase	phrase	pamphlet
phial	dolphin	nephew
triumph	sulphur	alphabet
elephant	telephone	graphic
telegraph	photograph	semaphore
graphite	Pharisee	pheasant
philosopher	gramophone	phonic
microphone	physic	

Teach:
When "p" and "s" start a word, the "p" is not "sounded".

"psalm" – "sarm"   "psychic" – "sykik"

Let the child use a dictionary to find other words.

29

SOME LAZY LETTERS

By this time the child will have met and realised that there are some words which contain letters that are not "sounded", e.g. knot, kneel.

Call them "lazy letters". The child will appreciate this.

It is not a wise plan to tell him that he must remember all the words with a lazy letter. There are far too many. Take one particular letter, list appropriate words, and let him *hear* them, *see* them, *say* them, *copy* them.

| *the lazy "b"* | climb | comb | crumb |
| | dumb | limb | |

| *the lazy "g"* | gnat | gnaw | gnash |
| | gnu | gnome | |

the lazy "gh"	high	sigh	light
	fight	night	might
	tight	sight	flight

| *the lazy "k"* | knot | know | knee |
| | known | knew | |

the lazy "l"	half	calf	calm
	balm	chalk	walk
	stalk		

the lazy "t"	often	soften	castle
	listen	bustle	whistle
	nestle	fasten	rustle
	wrestle		

the lazy "w"	wrap	wreck	wrist
	wrong	wrestle	wring
	wren	write	wrote
	sword	answer	

No spelling-bee – the child will soon recognise the words, given time.

30

WORDS SPELT THE SAME – BUT "SOUNDED" DIFFERENTLY

This is the final lesson.

If all the lessons have been patiently and correctly taught, with time taken over them, the reading ability of your child *must* have improved considerably.

There are some words which are spelt the same but are "sounded" (read) differently, and have different meanings. Do not go looking for them. Wait until they arrive, and the sense in the sentence will help.

For the last time I repeat, "Children are not stupid – they will learn if taught correctly."

A few sentences:

1. Have you *read* this book?
   Can you *read* this book?

2. The class made an awful *row*.
   We had a *row* on the river.

3. There was a long *tear* in this shirt.
   Alice watched the crocodile shed a bitter *tear*.

4. Robin Hood took his *bow* and arrows.
   The Sheriff was made to *bow* down.

31

SOME EXCEPTIONS
TO THE RULES

In almost every set of rules there are variations and exceptions – and there are many exceptions in the English Language, as you are no doubt aware.

Here are a few words which do not conform to the rules you have been teaching. Do not teach them as a lesson. Wait until the child meets them, and then take more words with the same exception.

The flow of words in a sentence helps the good reader – and your child should be able to take the exceptions in his stride.

The "long i"	bind	find	wild
	blind	child	mind
	rind	pint	kind
	grind		

The "long o"	old	told	gold
	sold	roll	cold
	both	fold	hold
	stroll	bold	scold
	bowl	flow	low
	tow	glow	crow
	own	flown	mow
	blow	grow	slow
	snow	throw	

The "short uh"	took	foot	cook
	book	hood	stood
	good	wool	

The "short eh"	bread	dead	head
	thread	stead	dread
	health	wealth	

Index

For easy reference, the first entry of each letter gives the page number for the "sound" of that particular letter.

Other titles in the same series:

THE CHILDREN'S PARTY & GAMES BOOK

There is no need to worry about hosting a children's party. Starting with planning the party and sending out invitations, Joyce Nicholson's book goes on to offer well over 100 different games to suit children of all ages, as well as other entertainments.

As an extra feature, she introduces ten themes for special parties, each of which is designed to make your child's party that bit different.

MAGIC MAGIC FOR ALL THE FAMILY

Geoffrey Lamb (an associate of the Inner Magic Circle) teaches how anyone (adult or child) can entertain family or friends with simple tricks and mysteries.

He presents over 50 tricks/puzzles – from delightfully easy, match tricks to more puzzling and elaborate card tricks. No complicated hand movements are involved or special props (just everyday objects such as: coins, newspapers, matches, handkerchief – for many you only need a pencil and paper) and the tricks don't need hours of practice!

To perform successfully, *confidence* is all. Learn how to gain it through the secrets of presentation which distinguish the accomplished conjuror. Hold your audience – yes – and hold it spellbound!

Uniform with this book

ELLIOT RIGHT WAY BOOKS, KINGSWOOD, SURREY, U.K.

OUR PUBLISHING POLICY

HOW WE CHOOSE

Our policy is to consider every deserving manuscript and we can give special editorial help where an author is an authority on his subject but an inexperienced writer. We are rigorously selective in the choice of books we publish. We set the highest standards of editorial quality and accuracy. This means that a *Paperfront* is easy to understand and delightful to read. Where illustrations are necessary to convey points of detail, these are drawn up by a subject specialist artist from our panel.

HOW WE KEEP PRICES LOW

We aim for the big seller. This enables us to order enormous print runs and achieve the lowest price for you. Unfortunately, this means that you will not find in the *Paperfront* list any titles on obscure subjects of minority interest only. These could not be printed in large enough quantities to be sold for the low price at which we offer this series.

We sell almost all our *Paperfronts* at the same unit price. This saves a lot of fiddling about in our clerical departments and helps us to give you world-beating value. Under this system, the longer titles are offered at a price which we believe to be unmatched by any publisher in the world.

OUR DISTRIBUTION SYSTEM

Because of the competitive price, and the rapid turnover, *Paperfronts* are possibly the most profitable line a bookseller can handle. They are stocked by the best bookshops all over the world. It may be that your bookseller has run out of stock of a particular title. If so, he can order more from us at any time – we have a fine reputation for "same day" despatch, and we supply any order, however small (even a single copy), to any bookseller who has an account with us. We prefer you to buy from your bookseller, as this reminds him of the strong underlying public demand for *Paperfronts*. Members of the public who live in remote places, or who are housebound, or whose local bookseller is uncooperative, can order direct from us by post.

FREE

If you would like an up-to-date list of all paperfront titles currently available, send a stamped self-addressed envelope to
ELLIOT RIGHT WAY BOOKS, BRIGHTON RD.,
LOWER KINGSWOOD, SURREY, U.K.